NOTES

ISBN 978-3-73923-843-2
Herstellung und Verlag: BoD – Books on Demand, Norderstedt
© 2016 Wolfgang M. Lehmer

Cover: modified Aprilia Habana 125 Retro   ArtWork by Owner: Wolfgang M. Lehmer

http://wolfgang-m-lehmer.de.to

Note, Date

Note, Date

Note, Date

Note, Date

Note, Date

Note, Date

Note, Date

Note, Date

Note, Date

Note, Date

Note, Date

Note, Date

Note, Date

Note, Date

Note, Date

Note, Date

Note, Date

Note, Date

Note, Date

Note, Date

Note, Date

Note, Date

Note, Date

Note, Date

Note, Date

Note, Date

Note, Date

Note, Date

Note, Date

Note, Date

Note, Date

Note, Date

Note, Date

Note, Date

Note, Date

Note, Date

Note, Date

Note, Date

Note, Date

Note, Date

Note, Date

Note, Date

Note, Date

Note, Date

address, phone, e-mail, homepage

address, phone, e-mail, homepage

address, phone, e-mail, homepage

address, phone, e-mail, homepage

address, phone, e-mail, homepage

address, phone, e-mail, homepage

password

password

password

password